Spanish Notebook

CHRISTOPHER BUCKLEY

Spanish Notebook

Copyright © 2017 by Christopher Buckley

All rights reserved. No part of this book may be reproduced or transmitted in any form or by any means without written permission of the author.

Author photo credit: Matt Valentine
Cover art by Nadya Brown, watercolor: *After a Mural in Oaxaca*

Library of Congress Control Number: 2017932027

ISBN: 978-0-9915772-7-9

Published by Shabda Press
Pasadena, CA 91107
www.shabdapress.com

Contents

Acknowledgments 1
Preface 5

On the Exhumation of the Poet 7
Homecoming, During a Storm 9
Sky Circling Among Branches 10
Photograph of Pablo Neruda, Chile, 1948 / Photograph of the Author,
    Eureka, CA, 1948 12
Concerning My Inadequate Education 15
Poem Beginning with a Phrase from Hernandez 18
Prodigal 20
The Way It looks 22
Saying 'Machado' to the Sea 24
Coplas 27
Grey Stars 29
Monday Passes 31
High Winds 34
Romancero 36
Dispatch from the Southern Provinces: 4th Year of Drought 39
Affidavit of Wind 42
Preguntas / Climate Change 43
Mitochondrial 45
Navigating in the Back Yard: Trying to View a Lunar Eclipse 47
On Hope 50
The Permanence of Elapsed Time: Reflections on a Parochial Education 52
Drought Season: Southern California 55
Working Sundays 57
A Little Knowledge 60
Beach Glass 63
Letter to the Sea 65
I Think About It 67
Useless 70
It Will Come to Pass in the Air 73
El Cielo 75
Walking Around 79
Soy el mismo hasta ahorra 82

Acknowledgments

Agenda	Poem Beginning with a Phrase from Hernandez
Alligator Juniper	Monday Passes
	Useless
ASKEW	Dispatch from the Southern Provinces
Birmingham Poetry Review	The Permanence of Elapsed Time: Reflections on a Parochial Education
Cloudbank	Navigating in the Back Yard: Trying to View a Lunar Eclipse
Evening Street Review	*Preguntas*
Fifth Wednesday	Saying 'Machado' to the Sea
	Working Sundays
5 AM	*Romancero*
The Georgia Review	Photograph of Pablo Neruda, Chile, 1948/ Photograph of the author, Eureka, CA 1948
The Harvard Review	Sky Circling Among Branches
Hotel America	Mitochondrial
	Letter to the Sea
Los Angeles Review	I Think About it
The New Guard Vol. VI	*Soy el mismo hasta ahorra*
New Letters	A Little Knowledge
	High Winds
The Normal School	On the Exhumation of the Poet
Parnassus West Review	The Way it Looks
Plume	On Hope
Poetry Northwest	Homecoming: During a Storm
Red Wheel Barrow	Beach Glass
Spillway	Drought Season: Southern California
	Affidavit of Wind
Stringtown	Grey Stars
Toledo Review	*Coplas*

Thanks, as always, to Gary Young, Jon Veinberg, and Nadya Brown for support and help with these poems.

Cover: Nadya Brown, watercolor: *After a Mural in Oaxaca*

*No hay nada major que las ocho
de la mañana en la espuma*

— Pablo Neruda

In memory of Luis Omar Salinas

Preface

This project came together in 2015 as I worked through a notebook of drafts, phrases, and lines from my readings of the great Spanish language poets, (as well as a few lyrics from popular Mariachi songs). I'd read several of William O'Daly's translations of Neruda's last books and had gone back to translations by Alastair Reid and Robert Bly. For most of my writing life, I have, like most readers of poetry, been captivated by Neruda's genius, but as well by that of Antonio Machado, Miguel Hernandez, and the generation of '27 in Spain, and of course César Vallejo. My friends Philip Levine and Ernesto Trejo translated the great contemporary Mexican poet, Jaime Sabines, in *TARUMBA,* and his poems were a catalyst as well. Together with a few earlier pieces, the book took shape over the next two years.

I am by no means fluent. I passed high school and college Spanish without distinction. A little over twenty years ago I was living in Menorca and had a thick edition of Neruda with me. I set myself the task of translating a poem each week, working only from the Spanish, my efforts regularly resulting in a poem a significant distance from the original, and I soon resigned from the ranks of fledgling translators. But my struggles with the Spanish had me closely checking the English against the original, and sent me to the dictionary for denotation and nuance to discover how the poet was charging his language, his vision. If nothing else, my efforts reinforced an appreciation of and enthusiasm for the brio, the voices, and imagery of Spanish poetry.

I jotted down lines in Spanish that I found especially resonant and inspirational. I made notations in English when I thought the Spanish might not later be readily remembered; I managed with a dictionary and a good degree of difficulty. Nevertheless, these poets provided energy, inspiration, and regularly jump-started my memory or sparked images that stimulated an emotion or event which threw light on a drifting passage or lead to a rough draft.

The presiding spirit over these poems is Pablo Neruda. No surprise there. Voice has been a major concern in my writing and reading for forty years or more; no one better than Neruda for the lyric intensity essential to producing a poem a reader can believe. Neruda's poems also inspired me to take risks, to look deeper into motivations, obsessions, ideas, fears, and language. All of these poets remind me, reinforce my belief, that human authenticity is paramount in a poem while coupled with imagination.

Finally, these are just my lyric poems, set largely in my home, Santa Barbara. The epigraphs at the top of each poem were the sparks, the signposts that set me off. The poems owe a large debt to these great poets. The cliché has it that *Poetry comes from Poetry* . . . and I am fortunate that in this case, no matter how modest the results, that is true.

On the Exhumation of the Poet

Isla Negra,
Chile, April 8, 2013

Mi deber es vivir, morir, vivir
—Pablo Neruda

As your body was lifted back into the air
Cellos and violins sang into the winds
From Antofagasta or from
The tattered sea or off the nitrate
Fields of Tarapaca, dead songs that come
To nothing. Your salted bones
Came back to testify against the black
Soul of America. What's left of you
Out on the steel table of cold causes,
Lost consequences, our history of lies?

*

The windows shook this morning
In southern California, the Santa Anas,
Hot from our deserts tore through
Eucalyptus, dry leaves. A few clouds
Stepped off the distance, white
As strips of gauze. No chance
Your odes will rise from the sea,
From solar dust, from mute eternity,
There's no chance your love songs
Will arrive on the burning winds,
A white ash falling from the sky.

*

The sea says nothing of another life—
Still, I want to taste the invisible
Savor of hope on the air, our common salt.
I want to hear your music
Beyond our blood. I'm waiting
For the winds to take up residence
Again in Santiago, Barcelona, or
Los Angeles, in sea foam, white caps,
To speak in the currents that drive
The waves, to tell us once and for all
That between here and the stars
No one gets away with anything.

for Philip Levine

Homecoming, During a Storm

Time lost its shoes
—Neruda

At 6, I was apprenticed to clouds,
and gulls sang out each grey decision
of the sea—
        I was content along side
the immense cold light, a string of stars
brushing the ocean's sleeve . . .
salt on the mist, the scent of eucalyptus
ascending the air.
        Of course
the fog moved in and took my place—
the spindrift of desire still slipping
beyond the breakwater . . .
and what knowledge was lost
in the blood, in the loose pages
of the waves, must have
been enough. . . .
        The trees
tip their green hats in time
with the erratic traffic
of my heart, the surf recites
its one rough prayer—
the words to which . . . the words
to which. . . .
        Nevertheless,
there's nowhere else
I'd rather be as the sky silts up,
as the horizon becomes obscure
as every thought I was ever sure of . . .
the harbor lights in a haze
as I walk along Shoreline Park,
waiting out the downpour
of the days left in front of me.

Sky Circling Among Branches

I'm coming, I'm coming, wait up, stones!
—Neruda

Good Pablo said the stones fell from the sky,
and science backs him up—all our beginnings
blasting out, clustering here or there
among the dark. . . .
              Whatever spun,
fell inward, and finally became us, amounts to
four or five like myself walking around
in the mornings with our ticket stubs
of intuition.
              October, a vacancy in the trees,
a couple rags of cloud caught up there, dingy
blossoms floating branch to branch . . .
                            and nothing—
not the perfection of the waves or the borderless
dominion of birds, not the Southern Cross,
that shimmering signet of hope—saves even one
of us in our sleep. . . .
              A night wind gallops
over the swells toward the islands at the end
of the sea. . . . Hands in my pockets,
all I turn up are keepsakes of dust,
the dulled archipelago of air stretching
beyond the tides.
              I go on, shuffling
down the path, whistling what was
once thought a lively tune, grateful
to be a satchel of ligaments and bone
still able to transfer enough chemicals,
one synapse to another, to understand
something is missing when I look up

and praise a streak of grey engraving
the hosannas of light, the spindrift
off the rocks, anything sent into the air,
post-dated to a god who,
in his infinite memory, must know
he's abandoned us here . . . so many
self-conscious bits of sand
in a starry whirlwind of desire.

Photograph of Pablo Neruda, Chile, 1948 / Photograph of the Author, Eureka, CA, 1948

The smell of barbershops makes me break out sobbing.
—Neruda

Old comrade, who needs a barber shop now?
Not me. And not you in 1948—the year
I was born, the year you were almost
already bald and most of who you would become—
except that it calls back a lost world
of Violet Water and Tres Flores, Lucky Tiger
and Bay Rum—a blameless childhood
savoring the glassy syllables
of the surf . . .
               What dreams were left
on the lips of the wind as you looked out
on the tender seas, on clouds that skimmed
the Pacific of nostalgia for the next 55 years
since this grainy snap, since you last thought
of a haircut?
               Sea-gypsies like ourselves
treasure whatever is thrown back by the tide,
each blurred chip of beach glass revealing
a misplaced scrap of light. We reclaim
that world dreaming of Vitalis, and Aqua Velva—
clippers humming behind our ears, thinning
shears clicking below the barbicide
in tall sea-tinged jars, talc descending
like cloud dust, and that blossom of alcohol,
mist of bloated roses, musty newspapers
and politics, standing chrome ashtrays
filled with sand, the stubs of White Owls,

Dutch Masters, and Muriel panatelas.
Argosy, LIFE, or the *Saturday Evening Post*
in the lap of an old-timer dozing
in the chair next to the john . . .
the slow blades of a ceiling fan churning flies
and the worlds we were losing in Temuco
and Montecito. . . .
                    You escaped on horseback
over the Andes, to Europe. I rode in comfortably
on the coattails of post-war economic recovery
on the northern California coast,
bald as a grape in my parents' baby pictures,
as you on your dust jacket photos. . . .
There I am, propped up and happy on the hood
of their new Pontiac, wearing a cap
the same as you'd wear the next 25 years,
and knowing, like you, the sound of the sea
before I knew my name, and 20 years to come
before I'd know yours . . .
                    Nevertheless,
here we are, preserved for posterity, the proletariat,
the glossy, on-going promotion of dust—you looking
young in middle age, younger than I've ever seen you,
younger than I am now—
                    sand-colored snapshot,
your short, steel-wool beard, the worker's shirt
and insubordinate look of a defender
of the oil-drowned seas, the clear-cut trees,
of the right of miners, of shovelers of nitrate
to sip at the honeycomb of oxygen—for which
they ran you out of the dining rooms of *caballeros*,
out of the Senate, for which they ate
their own words when yours made them infamous.
A few decades—out and back—*saludos*, and
adios.

  These photos recall that sleep-walking world
before each place was injured and improved,
before we were left with just snips of memory,
dreaming on opposite sides of the sky,
where there are no barber shops, no seats
in the cinema on Saturday afternoons,
no double feature and world news in black and white,
no wind-combed beaches reflecting the clear
thinking of the clouds.
      I never knew you
looked like this—hard, rough, defiant
as a root, spinning in place with the fury
of a water spout. I only knew the image
of a clean shaven, avuncular poet, bald
as a pope, but someone with rip tides,
the raging syntax of the ocean
up his sleeve.
     Who were we all our lives
ago, there on the edge of the sea,
the sky giving back our untroubled visions
in tide pools, in the resinous stanzas
of the pines? The fair weather clouds
floating our hearts as we headed off to school
each morning, stepping from stone to stone
on a path to the sky, where deep in the anonymity
of the air, we first and briefly were
whoever it was we said we were, Neftali Reyes!

Concerning My Inadequate Education

> *y ya ha pasado tanto tiempo*
> *que ya tal vez no existe nada,*
> *ni la pradera ni el ontoño*
>   —Neruda

I still don't have a clue as to the whereabouts
  of the linking verbs
that slipped out the classroom windows
  trailing the clouds . . .
as for the missing subject, the blank in the diagram
  on the board,
I was the last one to see it was You-Understood.
  I could never memorize
the catechism answers to *Who Made You?*
  Why did He make you?
Sure, I recognized the fluted columns of Persepolis,
  The Lighthouse at Alexandria
in our text, but that was ancient history even then,
  and nothing saved me
from staying after school to clap erasers, lost in a cloud
  of chalk dust
ascending all around me and numbing the air. . . .

I knew my rhymes, my two potatoes verses four,
  but was flummoxed when
it came to fractions, quotients, carrying remainders,
  but not by the long division
of afternoons waiting for the bell at 3:00 . . . by which time
  I'd not picked up
a single helpful hint from jays and mocking birds who
  answered back, rattled off
from the scrub oaks whenever the nun turned her back,
  and so set a bad example

for those of us in the back row whispering and trying
        not to get caught
passing notes and baseball cards to our pals during
        a rainy-day session
when the collective cloud of our breath fogged the windows
        like a plague out of Egypt.
Who could spell *transubstantiation* anyway? How in the world
        did St. Teresa levitate
by just skipping lunch and dinner? And that wasn't much more
        removed from the curriculum
than General Science where Lavoisier dismantled phlogiston
        in favor of oxygen,
both things invisible, so more to be taken on faith . . . the chemistry
        going on inside trees,
the multiplication tables of stars? How did our bones arrive
        from the trace minerals
of space? Do we return to an ossuary of light once time is up
        and the dust has settled?
Do we line up at arms' distance again and sing, or recite
        the usual creeds and
anthems regardless of fear and flames licking the dark?

The future? There wasn't one if we didn't solve the equation
        of Pagan Babies,
our weekly two-bit allowances dropped in a box
        for their admission
to the community of saints. The only problem I grasped fully
        was the holes in the bottoms
of my high top sneakers as I ran the bases or raced
        across the schoolyard.
I practiced penmanship, tried to work out the order of angels,
        but couldn't factor in
even one unknown and solve with any certainty for X.

The clouds never lost their way, and the birds, without
        ever stopping to think,
were never out of order in the air. Back then, in my white
        uniform shirt with stars
pasted on the collar for French, for Art, for my quiet
        comportment, I'd never
have thought I'd greet my remaining days without believing
        there was joy
to be had beyond the abandoned stations of the soul.

So much for my formative years—the question now is how
        to conduct myself before the wind,
the hearsay of dust, alone here, overlooking the sea?
        All I've managed
is to pick up the pocket change of fate when the leaves turn,
        my faith placed only
in smoke lifting each morning—my understanding never rising
        beyond the sky's blank sheet.

Poem Beginning with a Phrase from Hernandez

Future of all my bones,
fog too is dust. If the sea
has a soul, it's salt.

You can find all that
it comes to here—remnants,
clouds curled like boiled shrimp

above the coast line, tracing paper
on the blue, nothing written
beyond the insinuations of wind.

White gulls and godwits,
the invocation of the sun,
fair weather intimations that

I might come to something
before the light erases
every brown particular

from my childhood photos—
waving from my grandmother's arms,
holding onto her lilac farm dress,

onto the shell-shine of her face
from two centuries ago . . . .
Space streams away, constellations

like cells spinning their way through
the dark backgrounds of our blood,
like the clusters of larks

in Alondra Park that mourn
each evening with rondos
of notes grey as the horizon

disappearing over Point Arguello.
At last I know I am old,
that the sea is finally empty

of promises, though once
anything was possible,
as the ocean made its asides

to the palm leaves. Now I must be
content with next to nothing,
with the ribs of fish rolling

in the cradle of the waves,
with heaven weighing on my
shoulders like a wet wool shirt . . .

                      in memory of Ernesto Trejo

Prodigal

Es largo el tiempo, Pedro,
Es corto el tiempo, Rosa
          —Neruda

Turn back—
not one of your questions
was resolved beneath the sky
or moved off even a little
with the clouds. . . .
Any bird can read
the map of the air
to home.
          Weariness collects
with the dust in your cuffs,
dust that settles
each evening in the west . . .
what can it matter now
where you stopped
for soup, for bread?
Street sweeper,
sidewalk inspector,
bookkeeper of fallen leaves—
what choices are left?
The road ends in the sea,
the spindrift salt
drying on your cheek. . . .

Someone still needs
to make sense
of philosophy, to herd sheep,
to take in a stray cat.
Throw your arms up
in the face of the past,

little more now than
a fine powder on the path
leading to the edge of town
where no one expects you
on that bench outside the bar,
where someone stubs a cigarillo
and looks up through the smoke
to recognize the sack of hopelessness
slung over your shoulder,
the one you set off with
half full, half a life ago,
thinking there might be more
in the grab bag of the blue. . . .

Sit a while; sooner or later
they'll hand you a glass
of rough red wine
by the seawall there,
the fog hanging offshore
like the promise of a life to come,
a life just drifting off. . . .

Breathe in the mist,
the old uncertainty
grey as the pearl
of the sinking sun . . .
think of each misery
sidestepped, realize
how lucky you are to be
here with nothing left
but the empty light
of stars settling
calmly over the sea.

The Way It looks

un dia del cual tengo ya el recuerdo
—Cesar Vallejo

I'll be carried from the church of Mt. Carmel,
out the side door in the mock-adobe wall—
midweek, and the gardener sleeping through
lunch again, "Tu, Solo Tu" or "Cielito Lindo"
leaking from the radio in his truck . . . .
A day without even one witness
for the eucalyptus trees refusing
to rearrange a single leaf in loss.
                    An afternoon
of empty roads and pimiento boughs, some time
before the hills sink back into the Pacific,
and the Pacific into space—a day beyond recall
despite the lemon verbena and Bermuda grass
heavy on the air.
                    The classrooms will have
long surrendered beneath a veil of silt,
salt air smudging the windows, or is it a final
Bible History lesson hardly anyone learned
drifting off in chalk? Aleric, the last accredited
barbarian to ride into Rome, setting his example
of the passing and glory of the world. . . .
                            Equally,
the frayed rope ends of the bells, of the escaping
clouds—and the bundles of sticks I finally set down
among all my over-valued assets from the estate
of irony, that had theories for it all . . . purposeless,
in the end, as my brown shoes, as my mouth of ashes
kissing the butter-colored poppies, their bright
small fists shaking at the sky.

                        These are my personal
effects—the rain showers, the black & white light
of the '50s taken up in its faithful opposition
to the blue, to a heaven against which, even the wind,
for no apparent reason, was also driven to its knees.

Saying 'Machado' to the Sea

estos días azules y este sol de infancia
—Antonio Machado

It could be the blue wind
reacquainted with palms and cypresses,
or the running conversation
of the surf that has me less troubled now—
home to a small house on the cliff,
white walls dotted with red
geraniums, bottle brush, lime
and plumbago.
             I fill baths
and feeders for sparrows, towhees,
jays, and now spice finches
who have escaped the south,
the hard truth of the heat,
in their umber wings
and ash-colored waistcoats,
who fill the air with a high pitch
of praise and petitions.
             I too
am happy just to be here each morning,
piecing together whatever I can find
to live for, knowing there are
obligations to this glorious air
that fills my lungs each day
above the waves, even when
there's no music left
in the dry eucalyptus boughs. . . .

When a cloud passes over,
I recall my somber youth,
the companions with whom
I traveled this far, and wonder
what I have left to say
before the sea?
                    I no longer recall
a single one of my old poems
as I shuffle along with the dust in my cuffs—
dust, the one statement that endures. . . .
the one statement that endures. . . .
Yet, I can still recite by heart
Machado's lines about the battles
we have waged: *in dreams with God,
and awake with the sea. . . .*
I step a little outside myself . . .
the thin fabric of time little more
than the salt air between my hands
and lips. . . .
                    I recall his songs
of Castile, how he gave himself
to the common glories of the fields,
the lemon trees of Soria,
how all we are or have been
filters briefly through us
like light through a leaf.
                              Never mind
that it whips away in a gust, or
in the muffled tumble and fanfare
of surf as I look out beyond dusk
to bright flecks, the infinitesimal
reminders left overhead
in stars. . . .

He escaped Franco
and the Fascists, made it as far
as France where he died
three days before his mother,
where his last poem, approached
through memory, through dream,
was a blue bit of sky and the sun
of childhood on a folded page
found in his coat pocket.
Compañeros came by night,
crumbled pockets full
of Castilian earth over his grave
so that he'd be buried in Spanish soil,
said a final *coplas* in memory,
said his name quietly to the stars,
a name that helps me hold on
to the shirttails of the wind,
the name I say out loud fully
to the sea swells and the blue—
Antonio Cipriano José Maria y Francisco
de Santa Ana Machado Y Ruiz.
Machado.

Coplas

*So I go, drunk and melancholy,
lunatic guitarist . . .*
—Antonio Machado

White notes like bees, flicked strings of dust,
the air buzzes with wistfulness—a gypsy guitar,
a shipwrecked star silent beyond all birds . . .

in Menorca the old stone towers still reach
above the hills, a moon-white road drifting
off through a peristyle of clouds.

The sky is no longer on earth, where
it started as the misted breath of water—
a language we don't speak here anymore.

If there is a God who made all things—
comets, quasars, the sizzling galactic frittatas,
he had to know how lonely, in time, we'd be,

how the fingerprints of the dark would be
left around my wrists, and the lamp posts
along the breakwater would eventually all go out . . .

and instead of a love song, the dry afternoon
wind stutters in the eucalyptus, in an empty bottle
on the sill. Where will I get the courage

to throw myself to the fishes at this late date?
Your back always to the wall, someone is bound
to hand you a blindfold and a cigarette before long.

For the time being, I sit on a bench with a friend
enjoying a *robusto*, a *belicosa*, like some fallen king—
I'll be dead by the time it kills me . . .

I'm going back to green sea water,
that salt and sweetness left on the air
where I confess only to the ambiguous clouds.

Wallace Stevens, come out from behind the blue
palmettos, admit you were jack-lighting
the infinite for images, for the ligaments of belief.

When we're convinced that we are doing
important work, we're seriously in trouble.
Shepherds in the Andes have over 60 words

for the color brown in the coats of sheep.
If it's going to mean something,
it had better mean something . . . .

Grey Stars

Variations on a Theme by Machado

Ya la magica anguista de la infancia
La vigilia de angel mas austere
      —Antonio Machado

Evening glaze,
   impenetrable air of the past
      sifting through
the sieve of the sky
   before the light slips
      down
        overhead. . . .
For a time
   it all seemed as inexhaustible
      as the unmarked
margins of the wind,
   as my little prayer lifting
      and dissolving
with the spindrift
   before the sea,
     as an old
       picture postcard—
the horizon white
   beyond the cliffs. . . .
      On the theme
of an afterlife
   the sky's heard it all—
      hard this evening then

    to believe there ever was
                      an angel
                                watching over
                                              the sweet
anguish
            and intermittent bliss
                          of childhood—
                                      the bright inability
of the deep spangled blue
                      to tell us anything
                                  useful
about ourselves,
            the cosmos so nonchalant.
                            Nonetheless
it seemed reasonable to hope,
                    though there's not much left
to learn
          about wishes—
                    these sailing boats
                                  for instance,
with tangerine
            or lemon spinnakers,
                          working back
to the breakwater,
            were they ever headed anywhere
past these first grey stars,
                    their intermittent blinking
                                    in the great
equivocating sky?
            Sitting here
                    in my old canvas coat,
giving in to the gradual
                          interstellar drift,
                                the fact of the matter is
I correspond to them —
            unsure
                    as ever. . . .

Monday Passes

Sombra perdida entre las sombres,
—Jaime Sabines

Luna que se quiebra sobre
La tiniebla de me soledad,
A donde vas?
—Agustin Lara

Sabines said the moon can cure
an addiction to philosophy,
so I fell into bed late
between exhaustion and remorse . . .
other abstractions by then
having congregated in the park
across the street—indecision
on the edge of the picnic table,
arrogance pushing high on the swings,
self-pity following a hunchback
around the pond, Ego
clinging to the top rungs
of the monkey bars,
despair to the lower,
and so on. . . .

Outside my window,
sleep falls away leaf by leaf;
I am up drinking Saturday's coffee
with a teaspoon tarnished
as the minerals in my blood—
I salute the morning
clouds, wondering as always
what steps I can take to outlast them?
Place your bets! is all I ever hear.

I shuffle down the sidewalk
whistling *Noche de Ronda* as if
someone else were carrying
my dark star, lifting each uncertainty.
There must be a factory open all hours,
that ships out illusions, hopes
that spread themselves through
the streets at no charge. A time or two,
I threw myself into the waves,
but that got me nowhere beyond
a theory thin as an envelope,
that the soul might fit into.

By the windowsill, I sift through the dust
for clues . . always with the same
results—dust the prevailing condition.
Each afternoon, the on-shore breeze
comes up, and, any conclusions I have
come to, fly from my hands. The sea
shows no interest, but without it,
where would I be? Fountain pen,
duck-tail, switchblade, the artifacts
of youth tagged in the grey cells
with *Caramba!* or *Chingas Dominguez,*
echoing back there where we were
light-hearted, faithful
to the million small wings
revving in our veins
as if that was going to last forever.

No one heard God snoring,
though it seems likely now
whenever I listen to the tide
and try to scrape up the odds
and ends of meaning.
A dog will chew a dry bone,
dead—we used to say—
as a doornail
after he's dug all day.

There are never enough crumbs
brushed from heaven's tablecloth
to help those into whose hands they fall . . .
and there are always the handkerchiefs
the sky waves after you. . . .
I can't begin to count all
the metaphysical cufflinks
I've misplaced—there's no lock on the stars,
if that's where we fly off to?

I traveled to Venezuela
but never wrote a love poem—
the seabirds singing ode after ode
in the palms, so there seemed
no need to keep track. . . .
If night teaches me anything
it's to take whatever I can get
my hands on before I am a shadow
lost among shadows, and cannot
recover another miserable day.

High Winds

el cielo te chupa a través del tedro
—Jaime Sabines

Two con trails cross
like the tips of angels' wings
on the wind-washed blue—
a handful of clouds fans out
on the horizon—
pick a card, any card. . . .

Hope is like smoke—
I don't think I need
to explain that,
I try to recover some
old-school wistfulness,
anything that might
get me up and out
of the lawn chair where
I send *saludos* to the sky
any time something
up there moves.

I remember feeling the top
of my skull lift off
with heat or ideas, with love,
but I was 20-something,
and while it could have been
transcendental, a trans-
figuration among
the squash blossoms
and poles of runner beans,
I was likely skipping along
on the leading edge

of a chilled rosé,
hedging my bets
that someday I'd finish
deciphering psalms
in the dry sycamores,
faithful to the blur
from the thousand wings
moving, in those days,
through my blood.

Each year it appears
more certain that we will
not be saved, not be dropped
like envelopes, through
some high, invisible
slot, no glimmering
content, just the empty
white sides of our souls,
if even that much
of the metaphor applies. . . .

So why not live extravagantly,
place more geraniums
in the hanging baskets
on the porch even if
the magenta petals are bruised
and blown about all afternoon
and the only conclusion left
is that heaven has nothing
to do with any of it,
even if it feels that the light,
scouring and leveling the sky,
is sucking you up
through the roof . . . .

Romancero

I genuflect toward the sea.
                    —Luis Omar Salinas 1937-2008

No explanation
           in the stars,
                      the same staircase off the sea cliff
to the night . . .
           where else
                should we take up our lives a while?
All the archangels
           have taken the Greyhound
                      to Mazatlan,
except that old one
           smoking in his pick-up
                      in back of the church
in Robstown,
        Pedro Infante drifting
                  from the radio,
                            Bésame Mucho,
and *Tu, Solo Tu*
           infecting forever my Aztec, choirboy blood
                                 so that
I remember each Dolores
              on the promenade
                          infused with light,
the inescapable poverty of my pant cuffs,
                      every Mary and Martha,
the sorrowful mysteries
            of their necks.
                    A practical man at midnight,
I climbed the thorny bougainvillea
                  to balconies singing the salt air,
a pack of KOOLS,
            beer in a sack,
                  the articles of faith
                              as I knew them. . . .

I drove,
        one hand over an eye
                of my double-vision youth,
until my hat tipped
          and the ashes of moonlight tumbled out.
Beneath the apricot
        I unfolded each cloud,
                praised the small schisms
of the blossoms,
        of the soul on all fours
                as it floated away
with Paganini's violin concerto in D Major.
                Without so much
as a sandwich,
        I walked to Roeding park
                to learn what I could
from the larks about hope.
        All though the '80s
                I could tell
one neorealistic misery from the next—
                Visconti's from De Sica's,
the emotional sprockets and chain links—
                I knew there was
an hour missing in Bertolucci's *1900*,
            and long before that
I'd hit the road
        at the drop of a hat to eat rigatoni with Tony Quinn.
But finally there was
        no depth to the clouds,
                nowhere to bury
an angel's bones.
        I went back to the sea—my reservoir of dreams—
unfurled a white sail
        before the existential waves,
                but my heart
capsized in moonlight.
        I was a symbol
                of myself, an original
in Byron's sequined shirt,
        tip-toeing for years
                on the precipice

of the blue,
            in love with the undertow
                        of afternoon . . . .
Adios amigos,
            there is no melody left
                        to extract from the waves,
and the moon
            always did its best
                        to deceive me—the horizon remains
beyond eloquence.
            And if it takes a fool to be a poet, then
I've fooled no one.
            I went in search of roses,
                        not philosophy,
which I had
            freely from the sparrows in the back yard.
                                    I left
the sport coat of fame
            in the display window,
                        no inheritance
but the Latin invectives of the gulls.
                        I suppose there are
silver trumpets somewhere,
            and mariachis singing
El Rancho Grande,
            but I can't see them from here.
                                    My parents
took the package tour to paradise,
            and no doubt, put in a word. . . .
But God has a bad memory
            and is not sentimental.
                                    I bequeath
my manuscripts,
            illuminated and otherwise,
                        to the thrift shop
of the wind,
            and I will hitch-hike to the stars.
                                    You wouldn't think so,
but I loved God
            well enough
                        in my own way—
                                    what else
are the poor to do? And despite every opportunity
                                    he failed me.

Dispatch from the Southern Provinces: 4th Year of Drought

Yo soy un hombre literalmente amado
por todas las desgracias
—Blas de Otero

Sir: the barometers
of the dark are dipping,
but all that falls is dust
from the great indivisible. . . .
The rock of the sun remains
immovable. And despite the fact
that we crawled out
from beneath the waves,
we cannot drink the sea.
Once, clouds were black
stamps fixed to the pages
of a grey winter sky,
well wishers stood
at gravesides in a downpour.
Like table linen,
late spring moonlight
spread across the bay,
and in this way it was thought
a line of communication was open
with heaven—it turns out
we were just muttering
into the white caps tossed
nowhere by the wind.
                    Early on,
our time was spent indoors
memorizing times tables,
catechism answers, the spelling of
Antidisestablishmentarianism—

diagramming subjects and verbs
across the empty blackboard,
halos of chalk rising
over our heads as
we worked our way
to the illusive
predicate nominative
floating out there above
the ripe fields. . . .
Had anyone looked in
through the classroom windows
they would have seen us
fidgeting in our uniforms,
impatient at our desks,
our desire for the play yard
and drinking fountains
palpable as chalk dust
rising from the blackboard.

Now, all I know is that
the *comandante* kicks
his dog for chewing up
the yellowed newspaper
wrapped around the last shipment
of crackers and canned ham.
The public phones
haven't worked for years.
Nothing to do but sit
at my desk and look
through the filmed glass,
watch the ash drift by
spelling out our names
in cursive.
        The ocean has
endured all of us it can, and
though nothing was greater,
good Pablo told us,

than sea spray
at eight in the morning,
now it's stained with run-off,
clots of tar thick as grief
floating on the oil-slicked swells.
There's no escaping our
investments in greed,
the residual misfortune.

One or two clouds
are just empty boats, sailing off
for the outskirts of light—
I walk the perimeter, stop
and cup my hand to my ear,
but do not hear the first syllable
of wind—it's useless inside
this shell of parched air. . . .
Over time, time is of course
involved; the meteorologist
repeating himself about cycles
in the official communiqué.
But as my last posting said,
it's all dust here, polished
by the boundaries of fire.
All I have to report,
the only conclusion available,
is that God never had any
intention of coming back
to see what we've done
with the place.

Affidavit of Wind

Me dormi esperando el otoño
—Neruda

Only the framework of light, the syntax
of dust, to interpret evening's edge
shifting blue and electric above the cliff line,

bivouacked between whatever's behind
the galaxies' un-spun threads and
the free association of atoms consigned

to the distance, where gravity, where desire,
barely obtain. Given the timeline of cosmic grist,
the air thinning steadily over the Himalayas,

the alibi of the heavens doesn't come to much.
In the eucalyptus, doves again evaluate
the hopeful repetitions of leaves—why not

turn to the wings lifting off as evidence
of everything beyond dusk? The cemetery
on the cliff overlooks the sea's grey slate—

the markers and the waves, swept clean
of dreams each day, the undercarriages of clouds
strung along, one embedded ellipses at a time. . . .

Preguntas / Climate Change

Preguntamos, y morimos

Me parece conocer a Ud.
No es Ud. un contrabandista?
—Neruda

How many doorways
                have I looked into
                                to find no one
home,
      no one waiting
               for me to pass
                         the time about rain
that never falls
         on cabbages, artichokes,
                      sea-dull acacias,
the sun-scraped lawns?
                Dirt scurries this way then that
on the walk—
         what can you do?
                    In my old school photograph
there's a grey cobweb
            of the soul
                  in the background,
and, little more than silhouettes,
                        who doesn't see that the trees
lining the cliff
          have given up,
                  that the sky looks tired
of everything?

Who said
      the rain calls out the dead—
                          but how in the world
would we know now?
                What good are all the hosannas
sent by sea birds
            to the limit of the stars?
                        The night holds its breath,
barely keeps back
          the empty showcase

                              of oblivion.
I look around
            and get the distinct impression
                                    no one remembers
a thing,
        not the nickel-colored clouds of 1956,
                                    not Eisenhower
and Konrad Adenauer,
                and everyone who saw it coming
by the boat load,
            who stood there
                        and did nothing,
                                    as a post-war
economy built more bombers, Buicks, and TV trays,
                                but didn't
toss a potato peal
            to the half of the world
                            who died,
                                    who did the work.

Who routinely stepped into the other room
                                as the kick-backs and dividends
from take-overs, sell-offs, and insider trading
                            were slipped
into the suit pockets of congressmen, and CEOs,
                                who, for everything
it was worth,
            churned the atmosphere
                            like investment accounts—
every molecule
            thickening the portfolios
                            of breath, here to Bejing?
You can watch
            the glaciers
                        melt on a web cam—
                                    and the rising
sea level, doesn't that speak to
                        something fairly immediate?
There are no new clouds.
                How bright do you have to be
to see that the sky has it in
                    for every one
                                of us who isn't smart
enough to call out the sneak-thieves
                            and industrial smugglers
who are filling our hands
                with more dust,
                            with the final extortion
of the air?

Mitochondrial

hasta darnos la suma
de la totalidad de
infinito . . .
—Neruda

The wind may still be outside the Arlington Theater, holding my jacket after the Saturday matinee—I forget exactly where I left it—but everything adds up eventually somehow, according to atomic theory. . . .

At night, I hear the coyotes from the mesa, last of the romantics, howling, *Love, Love, Oh Careless Love*, whether there's a moon or not. I lie awake, the lost stars out there grazing in the blue night over the foothills, where I'll never find my way back. But I recognize half a dozen clouds that have tracked me down with that vague grey weight from childhood. Clouds improvise and it's hard to tell, but I know them. And the galaxies, strung across the night like chicken wire, though moving away from us, aren't going anywhere.

I want to say the eucalyptus trees consider the wind a necessary annoyance, an outright provocation, but I'm projecting—I say things and hope they add up. In California, honey bees are literally disappearing into the blue—lost, dying, and it might be cell phone signals crisscrossing and interrupting their homing radar—or a virus—default biology. The farmers and those of us that eat are worried about pollination, the lack thereof, the road to rock, sand, our witless ruin, or Riverside where there is always drought.

Some still believe crop circles are extra terrestrial—not due to the British blokes who admitted to having everyone on. There are still votes for animal gods, and one god that covers everything with seven orthodox days of intelligent design. Pick any leaf and it's more complicated than that.

Everything happens because of what you did before, but this is just cellular degeneration, planned obsolescence, not reincarnation, not a reason why we're here. Not another *Jeopardy* question about the CERN particle accelerator—is it in France or Switzerland? The positrons collide on the border, but that doesn't tell us where the clouds go. I'm always looking southeast over the sea. Like everything, clouds probably keep circling here, charging into our breath, working along in formation in our blood from thousands of millions of years back, where the scientists think the mitochondrial DNA hopped off a comet and got in the swim.

The nuclear quotient and codes from interloping bacteria slowly, gradually, accounted for us, our bright and promising futures, and eventually for me walking down the hall in the middle of the night wondering where I'm going . . . and soon I'm walking past the old storefronts down town on State Street, the Woolworth's turned to a bookstore, to sporting goods, to a café. But it's the same gilt-edged glass that caught and released my image, age 5, tagging along with mother to the shops.

    The windows do the same today, in a million specks of light, my grey image imprinted on the sky, which may be all we have when it comes to the sum total of infinity.

Navigating in the Back Yard: Trying to View a Lunar Eclipse

> *Pro fin despues de navagar*
> *llego adonde yo me esperaba.*
> —Neruda

Between the tool shed
                 and the liquidambars,
                              between
the marine layer and the rising night,
                          I discover nothing
more than time passing above the patio,
                             strips of dark wind
among the leaves—
             squalls of light moving
                              to where ever
it is light moves off to
              when it's done
                       with us. . . .
                                 In 5th grade,
our Geography teacher,
           Miss Vasquez, told us how Magellan,
sailing the straights
             of Tierra del Fuego,
                        saw the fires
of natives
       on cliffs at night
             and thought the stars
were descending,
          burning down the sky. . . .
                            Out here,
on a far arm of the Milky Way,
                    we are marooned among the stars,
just a bit
        of the 4 & ½ % of things glimmering
                               anywhere—
an infinitesimal flare
            among the indifferent
                         mathematics

of the dark.
     At Point Conception, the waves line up
               like
so many empty pews in church,
         and against the horizon
I see a thread of smoke lifting
        into nothing
             from a parking lot
trash fire—
    broken glass sparkling
         like sugar
             or the pinwheeling
frenzy of molecules spread
        from the initial inferno . . .
and who knows when
        the next meteor will escape
             and streak
the interstellar hanger dome of night,
         briefly flagging
our attention. . . .
     A few years back,
         a Russian satellite
tightroped
    the hypotenuse of space,
          a golden string dissolving
directly above our house.
      Down the hill,
         lights of the shopping center
float all hours
    on the dark,
       and there are more than enough electrons
to keep ads whirling,
     popping up on the internet
          unanswered
as our response
    to the signal
       from around Sagittarius
            that SETI
researchers at Ohio Sate detected in 1977,
        sure it was a message
from extra-terrestrial intelligence.
        The end of September, 2015,

I sit out waiting,
            looking up
                        to follow the last full lunar eclipse
until 2033,
            not knowing
                        if I'll be thinking anything
                                                by that time?
The moon goes orange,
            then a smoky garnet red—
                                    as if on fire,
rising over the cliffs
            above my head.
                        When did I ever think
of light as anything
            but timeless
                        relative to the rest of us
walking around
            a while in our t-shirts and running shoes,
picking up shells at low tide,
                        absentmindedly humming
a faint melody,
            that undertow
                        in our blood phased
like sea swells,
            each deep
                        ocean current, unseeable wave
of gravity
      going through us,
                  as we arrive where
we always expected to—
            headlong into the vast
and unaccountable. . . .

On Hope

Yo me perdono da saber
Lo poco que supe en mi vida
   —Neruda

Old school, old soul, still writing with a fountain pen—standing by
  the wobbly splendor of the sea
with light dwindling westward . . . I'm trying to work something out
  without pointing to the longhand
of the stars again as the place we'll likely end up. Each evening,
  I have nothing to ask the heavens for
more than time, as, with wind rattling the eucalyptus, I recognize
  another voice lost among the leaves. . . .
And if I stick my head out the window, I can sometimes hear
  that old socio-economic blues
still pulsing above the avenues of New York, where I was let go
  with no idea where I'd work
the following week, where I sat in an audience after my last shift
  and they weren't about to let me
back stage to sip white wine with Samuel Becket and talk
  the Theater of the Absurd
as he waited to go on Dick Cavett. So I hedged my bets
  about St. Michael, all the angels
and Union Reps manifesting above the Verrazano Narrows
  in Versace robes. 20-something,
my imagination still unchecked, but I found some consolation
  in Pablo chewing out the old poets
in floppy ties for investigating their own tender emotions
  and never writing about
longshoremen, bus drivers, or seamstresses who need more
  than a half-hour lunch
and payroll savings plan, who ignore pain in their knees and sacroiliacs,
  pain of rents and car repairs,

of scraping together a sack of groceries walking home beneath
        their defeated stars—who never
had a minute off to ask if there was meaning in suffering.

    And what then to do with philosophers?
Nietzsche—with his Zoroastrian dancing star, his fateful roundelays—
        is only a poet, crazy-ass as the next one.
His *Eternal recurrence* just keeps the wheels spinning—everything comes
        to nothing, a subatomic particle at a time. . . .
Our parochial bowl of light overflows with mystical second guesses—
        no one carries a star in their heart. Add a zero
to the cloud count and see if you're carried off day-dreaming above
        the foothills. I've lapped myself with speculation,
copied out my lessons with no chance of diagramming our atoms
        in the run-on sentence of light—a bit
of silver at the horizon's stormy edge is all the circumstantial evidence
        of an afterlife you'll find. At dusk, it's only
finches arguing in the air, descending from nothing more than the high
        and vacuous burden of the sky. . . .

What more do I have to rely on? The birds ignore me until the feeder
        runs out, then shoulder in expectantly
despite the sparse evidence to be found each day, most of which
        once it's set before us, is erased,
obliterated, or simply escapes our notice. What does it finally matter
        what we want, the Buddha says?
And though I forgive myself for knowing what little I've known in my life,
        I watch a star break loose and
shoot across the night—and based on that, I'm supposed to have hope. . . .

The Permanence of Elapsed Time: Reflections on a Parochial Education

My soul is a burned log...

*... in the trains that passed through my childhood
beneath the green hands of the rain.*
—Neruda

Rain all through childhood,
                                  grey days like sheets on a laundry line
hanging above our heads,
                 and no secrets to keep
                                        from the sky....
Light died
         into the sea,
                 and there was no reason to believe
                                              that anyone
would intercede
              and save us
                      from the pale kingdom of bone
whose talismans clicked around
                               the dark necks of the nuns.
We copied out one chapter after another
                                      but everything disappeared—
hobby shop and soda fountain,
                       boardwalk and department stores,
corner mom-and-pop
                 with circus-colored jawbreakers,
Abba-Zabbas, and Zero Bars.
                     I was left with an attic trunk,
a few goose feathers
                floating out of a Golden Book
                                  the clockwork
of waves....
            Driftwood fires on the beach,
                            smoke dissolving

on the shoulder blades of a breeze,
         the dark flames of cypress
against a horizon that spread like a blood stain
            over the blue. . . .
Whatever it was I wanted,
       there was nothing in the North Star,
the Corona Borealis,
     or the commercial light of Christ . . .
far too many memories
     to put together
         before they drifted off
like clouds, obscure in the distance,
       and I was back where I started.
When I look up
   I have to think
      that the hat makers of eternity
need to ask themselves
      what use they've been on earth?
We're uncovered as rabbits
      running beneath the moon,
counting on the one-time capacity
     of our blood
        to calm us
in that pause, that minute before
       the question mark of dusk
darkens, and I've nothing left to do
      but take silence by the arm
and walk it around the block again,
      shake my head and whistle
my way along
   as if I were out of complaints
       and my brain
had been battered by the firmament a final time.

When I head to my back porch
      and a chair angled
        so I might be
acknowledged by the cosmos,
     by stars in their dazzling
         hexagrams,

in the unsolved equation
                        of space, nothing points toward where
each bright bit is heading
                        while there's still time.
                                              For now,
it looks like my best chance is
                        to genuflect once more
before the waves
                        and make the sign of indifference
                                                across
the forehead of the night.
                    Why would it to add up to more
than sea foam,
            saltwater murmuring in my veins
                                      no matter
how many times
          I call in to the office managers of misery,
leave a message
             with the temporary assistants of misfortune
asking where my name is on the list?
                            If I have a soul,
its a veil of rain in a virelay
                    from the19th century.
Chances are
          I won't receive any more consideration than
the spindrift, the smoke
                 from the last burning log
                                       on the beach—
the seconds flying off
             to nowhere,
                          sparks fizzing out
against a sky that's nowhere close
                        to solving the problem
of my cells' standing invitation to oblivion,
                                  like that echo
of the train roaring out of town
                    regardless of how many verses
of old school hymns
                  we send out on the brief toccata of the stars. . . .

Drought Season: Southern California

> *. . . hasta quando*
> *el paraguas de Baudelaire*
> *nos acompaña a plen sol?*
> —Neruda

Each day now
      before I go out,
           I put on an old straw hat
so the little hope I have left
      does not evaporate
           out the top
of my head. . . .
      My umbrella knits cobwebs
           behind the door
as I pass the dry roadside trees
      and can't help but think
of Goya's *El tres de mayo*,
      how, with their arms surrendered
to an empty sky,
      the soldiers look just like those trees,
           slumped
into each other, waiting to be shot. . . .

I know a bougainvillea
      that's still making a heart-red run
through the prickly pear
      on the cliff—
           most mornings
that's enough to get me out,
      have me toss yet another
worthless prayer past the islands,
      the crags of Santa Cruz,

the far reaches
            of San Miguel,
                        looking for any trace of cloud
edging in
        from 60 years ago . . .
                        2nd grade, and a steady drizzle
tasting of salt and iron
                each morning as I stepped from the bus.
I wore a blue school sweater
                    over my skeleton suit
that Halloween
            as we paraded around the courtyard
even though
        mist continued to fall
                        on tables of cup cakes
and jack-o-lantern cookies. . . .
                But daydreaming
is so much dust
        in the rain barrel
                    rusted at the corner
of the house—
        still, I think of the B westerns filmed
just 90 miles south,
            the ones we watched
                        every Saturday morning
in black & white
            while it rained,
                    while the clouds of dust were rising
from the posse in pursuit. . . .
                What chance now
                            the sky's
going to open up
            and return us to those days?
                            Above the bay
each evening, there's just that cloud of dust,
                    the starlight blurred,
burning down. . . .

Working Sundays

de tanto arar, el sello triturado
de nuestra pobre eternidad terrestre
— Neruda

I decide to sit down beside
the abandoned offices of the sea,
the spray's salt bite dissolving
with my thoughts into the sky,
empty now of a future
but where there's always more
to worry about if you look
for it. . . .
        My white shirt
whips in the wind, and
I can hardly remember
the last time I clipped on a tie—
but like the Herman's Gulls
loitering in their old grey coats
above the tide, I'm not late
for anything, not going
in to work . . . so if there's something
I still owe, a balance left in some account,
I can't imagine what it is,
let alone give a good rat's ass. . .
there's nothing left
they can do to me now.

I pick the pockets of a cloud
or two that don't notice me here
in the shadow of the palms,
grey as a little water leaking
from the sprinkler line.
I'm going to do nothing
but admire the spendthrift light
dawdling across the advancing
afternoon, out over the western edge
of space.

          Working all those years
who could afford any evil ways?
And now that I just might,
my body can't tolerate a bump
in blood pressure or one
miserable bit of carbohydrate.
I could care less if I get a bad name
from the Better Business Bureau
sitting here all day, scarcely distinguished
from the homeless who can barely help
themselves let alone the deserving
black birds bivouacked by the bins
amid sandwich wrappers and
a minor kingdom of crumbs.

Bet high and sleep in the streets,
was my motto, especially
for the job fairs with their epaulets
and elbow patches. No one cared
if I took my knocks, if the soles
of my wingtips, which I helped myself
to at the Thrift, were worn through.
They were Florsheim Imperials,
and still sported the pattern of small holes
on the toes and sides reminding me of stars,
or more usually that something was missing.
What could I do but to put it down
to experience, get off the elevator
holding my book bag like every other
sucker at the no-host bar who
expected rewards in proportion
to the hours put in?
                        I got my start
working Sundays, mopping floors
at dawn, then unloading trucks until
I found myself on my knees stocking shelves
with peas, beans, pickled beats and
every other processed product in a can
while the subliminal messaging
of the Junior Chamber of Commerce
oozed across the buffed linoleum
on the cascading strings of Montovani—

background Muzak guaranteed
to provide happy shoppers. And Jesus,
Charlie Cantello is still chasing me
down Milpas Street in my dreams,
yelling that I'm late for my shift
and didn't I check the schedule?

I still remember my days off,
days I could camp in my van
at the beach without being rousted,
and wake up to tumbling lines of surf,
wax my long board and hit the tubes
praising creation as a translucent lip
of a wave sang back the glory of the sea. . . .

I'm going to clock in regularly now
on this bench— the price is right,
the hours are great—I'm going to
get out and walk along the path
through the park, wear down
the waffle tread on these old Nikes
before I find myself stumbling
along the sidewalk leaning on a zimmer.
I've put in my time and now
it's too late to rush. . . .

There's little to do but hold on
as the universe unfolds before me,
just like Einstein who predicted
gravity waves 100 years ago this week,
part and parcel of a unified field.
And yesterday, physicists finally
located them rolling though
our neighborhood, and that's what I call
staying on the job. I doubt if
it's going to help with the HMO deductible
or cost of living raise for social security,
and I'm pretty sure it will have
no beneficial effect on life extension?
But there's nothing else left to do
except sit here and relax, wait
for the next thing to come along
and hit me out of the blue.

A Little Knowledge . . .

            y entre los que menos sabian
            yo siempre supe un poco menos
                —Neruda

I was always a dangerous man . . .
                among those who knew things,
I always knew
      a little less,
           the sky offering nothing
                  in exchange
for my dumbfounded interest.
        I dug holes at the beach,
                poured in
seawater, and, as it drained,
        looked up wondering . . .
                above me,
the blank sky
    waiting to be filled in—
            come sun, rain, or fog,
come the salt air, the momentary
        foolproof joy of my days.
In college,
    I looked out the window,
            put in the requisite hours
of confusion—
    daydreaming, alas, was not
            a curriculum choice. . . .
There I was, staggering out
        of the St. Francis in San Francisco—
haircut, sport coat, tie,
        drunk as a lord on gimlets,
                without a worry
for an hour or two,
    knowing my way to Union Square
                for a cab,

knowing just enough
                for my gentleman's C
                                  which kept me in school,
out of the draft
                and jungles of Vietnam.
                                    It didn't matter then
which blind date had left me
                on the dance floor—
                                there was death
to dodge in the immediate forecast,
                      exams in the Presocratics
and accounting,
            disputes
                    about beauty, the origins of meaning,
none of which were resolved
                          in trigonometry where I hung on
by one abstruse thread after another,
                          understanding only
that sine, cosine, tangent—
                  such coded, quantifiable abstractions—
would in no way contribute
                to my life. . . .
                              And here I am, almost
a lifetime later
          seeing I was right for once—
                          the crumbled geometry
of mountains
          ending in the sea
                as I investigate
                        the white sky,
the square root of space
              filled with silence,
                          something I can prove
each morning as I step out
              with nothing
                        on my mind—one chapter
after another written on sea foam,
                  rising into the air.
                              I don't ask

much more than that . . .
                         some seagulls, reaffirming the air
still supports life,
             do not need me
                            to explain
                                       what they're up to
while I walk along
                   waiting for something
                                         besides dust to settle. . . .
It's too late
           to do much
                     but pull up a chair
                                        and declare astonishment.
I've tracked a cloud drifting
                             behind the tangled branches
                                                        of liquidambars,
highlighting,
            as far as I can see,
                                one crooked path of reasoning

after the next.
              Across the street,
                                the three-legged dog pees
on the neighbor's dahlias
                         and happily hobbles back to his yard.
Stars are spinning away up there
                                but seem to be in the same place—
sprays and swirls,
                  and it looks like
                                    the accounts can't be balanced.
I might as well whistle
                       after the birds
                                      winging north
                                                    and think
I understand.

Beach Glass

Perdon si por mis ojos no llego
Mas claridad que la espuma marina
      — *Neruda*

The tides grind out beach glass as if
  it were nothing . . .
and it is, except that we gather chips
  and glimmerings
from the sand, raise them against the light
  and look back—
some small piece of our lives at the end
  of our fingertips,
lit and holding still a moment . . . a chunk
  of Coke bottle
from the '60s, green and vague as the air
  before a storm,
or a shard opaque as smoke, as the fine
  powder of the past. . . .
trailing me like ash from autumn fires
  falling across the hills . . .
salt winds shifting my mind's loose straw. . . .

  Every few years
I find myself looking out from here,
  thinking I finally see
things clearly . . . on the horizon another layer
  of haze appears
to have been wiped from the window frame.
  Infinity's out there
and no one can turn away. A fanfare of leaves
  is pushed about

by a thoughtless bit of breeze, a sandy blur
 of glitter riding
the evening dust . . . and here I am
 with a fog-white chip
held to my eye—everything behind me now
 just that clear. . . .

Letter to the Sea

De tu casa a la mia
Cielito lindo, no hay mas que un paso
—Quirino Mendoza y Cortés

Today, I am hand-delivering my reply, my aggregate dispatch of grief, my near-sighted thoughts. No great distance between us now. You knew I was coming all along. My mystery novel unopened on the bench, I've given up trying to unpuzzle the evaporation of time, something you know all about—salt from spindrift to air—because now, as I see it, there is little more to do than sit here, counting the lines of surf, the indeterminate subatomic scramble, the foam that might be all we are. . . .

As a child, I sang to you in Spanish, practicing *Cielito Lindo* for our summer parade—*Sing don't cry* was the refrain, *Canta y no llores* . . . a lesson repeated *ad infinitum* for my elucidation, like Latin in parochial school—*stella, stellae, stellae* . . . the cold declension of the stars, or *Sic transit Gloria mundi*—and by now we all know what happens to the glory of the world.

And so just downhill from the elementary school, I let the thick steam of cafeteria lunches wash over and carry me away—macaroni, boiled green or lima beans, fish sticks, stew . . . the pasty aroma of the past rising to the clouds, and the clouds bouncing along the mountain crest of the Santa Ynez as they did 60 years ago when I was released for recess and watched them sail white as Ivory Soap Flakes toward the shore.

None of this is news, but as far back as I remember you have been a reliable correspondent, and this is the avocation of age where we are steadily called away from the world, and these are my notes in ink blue as the Pacific. They are not regret, nor the scrap heap of expectations, or even loss particularly, because that is everywhere. . . . And though I keep sweeping out the hallways of the past, it is not the abstractions of Faith, Hope, and Charity drilled into us long ago that concern me. Rather, it's something indefinite, unreadable, closer to mist, to the smoke from the robusto I am not allowed drifting off to wherever it was Faith and Hope and even the angst of middle age disappeared to—just one more thing questionable, wind-sprung among the acanthus and madeira here at cliff's edge.

I've filched a few canna lilies from the small park to stand in for the sun, but they have not improved my disposition. The fog rolling in concentrates the mind and I recall that the Assyrians always descended upon the plain, that all of us have suffered. Still, I reflect each day on the silky great grey coat, the numinous eyes of my cat, Cecil B, taken unawares by cancer long before he'd finished his appraisals of the garden, the sky, and every corner of our household. His absence is the question I send out each day, floating on the last ash of the horizon—inside my overcoat, will I find a soul, however grey, any address, any rendezvous for our dust down the fading light?

How can I be content with a boatload of improbability arriving with each wave? Each day now is like a test day, one for which I never adequately prepared, given my talent for wool-gathering, for looking back down the road at dusk. . . . The gulls know what to make of the mist and wait it out in small flocks, and perhaps that is instructive, and all the reply I will receive? I note finally the calm and quiet susurrations of the surf, the spare texts on hand for consolation, for any basis of airy speculation. I pass these insubstantial pages to you, my friend, this side of the sky.

I Think About It

ay ese mundo es la victoria,
es el paraiso perdido
—Neruda

Out in evening fog,
        it's the only relief
                against four dry years . . .
like a bell in a church,
        I pull on the grey rope
                of the sky, trying
to figure out this calculus of dust,
        the brambles, the broom straw
of light . . .
        stars burning all this time for no one?
                And the implications
of dusk?
      They look hopeless as well,
                but there should be something.
Not that long ago,
        I was running around on my grandparents' farm
catching fireflies in my bare hands—
        hands the cosmos gave me
to wave
      at assemblies of clouds,
              at the passing infinites of air.
At my desk
      with a box of crayons and construction paper,
                I was ready
to make something
      from next to nothing
                when the nun clicked

the Motorola on
>for the *Standard School Broadcast*
>>so we might,

all preconceptions aside,
>slipstream with whatever rose

off the glorious sea swell
>of the orchestra. . . .
>>Now I content myself

with a mocking bird,
>his jump-cut notes from the telephone poll,

calling, like me,
>for some explanation
>>of the situation. . . .

Reviewing the choices,
>I shrug my shoulders and shuffle along

leaving the guesses,
>the cart load of ironies, to whomever believes

he can make sense of them?
>If I have a soul I should worry about,

it's the next thing to spindrift,
>a little sea salt
>>dried on the rocks. . . .

Home, I sit in the kitchen,
>keeping company with a glass of red wine—

I might as well invite
>the silence in to take a chair,
>>see which of us

remembers how hard it rained back there
>as I ran with a newspaper

held over my head
>to the miserable jobs of my youth
>>thinking

things couldn't get any worse . . .
>or see who recalls the snow falling

in the Dark Ages of our History books,
>a courtyard by an abbey,

some beggars and back-alley heretics gathered
                                around a small fire,
behind them
            a few bones tossed
                            for the priests' dogs,
                                            gleaming
on the dark stones
                like stars. . . .

Useless

Perdon a todos por innecesario
—Neruda

Whenever I step out, the wind searches my house,
        drawers, cupboards,
bookshelves, and turns up nothing but the dust
        it found last time through . . .
a few incomplete sentences about what might be beyond
        scattered on my desk.
The newspaper hits the porch with a story about
        a new invisible planet,
its gravitational tug ghosting Kuiper belt debris . . .
        an ice giant, a dark bend
in gravity—10 x the size of the earth, 20 x farther out
        than Neptune—15,000 years
for 1 revolution about the sun. Sorry to miss you—
        catch you next time around?

As a child, I watched the slow boats of cumulus chug by . . .
        there was nothing else
to do but stand on the cliff with my useless wonder
        like some outlaw in a western
dropping the loot, hands up, reaching for the sky.
        I leave the window open
in case there's the least insinuation of salt air
        through the eucalyptus leaves.
Let me get to the point here . . . the hours keep moving
        like schools of fish
in the sea, and somewhere there's a net in the background
        glaze of galaxies that stops
time, every thought and memory blurred as stardust sifting
        down to us all these years.

The winds are blowing hot again here on the coast,
        so no one cares
if I stroll the breakwater mumbling along with the tide
        and the liturgy of waves,
waiting for the sky to open and the voice of Chuck Heston
        or Cecil B. De Mille
to break through. Daydreaming's got me to a point
        where I have nothing left
in my pockets but my imagination, a handkerchief
        which I can wave
all day at the sky and produce the same results. . . .

        Back in my hell-fire days,
I worked every Sunday, and what did God do? He slept in
        as always, breathing out twisters
across Oklahoma, hurricanes that pummeled the Philippines,
        never minding how many houses
were reduced to twigs or who slept in the streets, let alone who
        went to 10:00 mass,
who boxed groceries, washed cars, or tuned-in The Game of The Week.
        At the lunch tables
Eddy Villa-Señor ate baloney on Fridays instead of tuna and
        was never struck down.

When the fog rolls in I wrap a scarf around my neck and walk
        about trying to remember
anything that's still important? Time's almost up . . . if there were
        warnings of trouble
to come, they were ignored as we shoved everything we could
        into our pockets
as if our cells were going to outlast the light. Nevertheless,
        I contribute so little
to the landfill now that from any bench I feel I can lift
        my arms into the air and be
justified saying, Not me, my hands are clean. All I have
        to pay back are

a handful of indifferent phrasings filched from the blue.

      The conifers climb
hand over hand into the sky, stars swim past my fingertips . . .
      every galaxy's redshifted
and moving away from us as fast as it can—and what are we
      going to do about that?
I gave up counting summer stars half a lifetime ago
      and made my argument —
for what little it's worth—about how short eternity is
      here on earth.

It Will Come to Pass in the Air

Ha de ser en el aire:
Un mundo
Donde yo llego a respirar con todos
Mis silencios acordes.
—Jorge Guillén

At the kitchen table I look up
to the ceiling and sigh—
running through rows of solitaire,
I realize I'm using up
whatever luck I have left. . . .
The sky here doesn't change much
day to day but I am one of those
who shines his shoes every Monday
in case something turns up,
in case the jet stream swings down
our way again with rain—
who for hors d'oeuvres
has crackers and tinned sardines,
knowing it costs something to grow old,
knowing there are miseries stored
in the attic, the roof mortgaged
to the blue.
      We're here, then
we're not. I walk in the fog
and keep my head down, and
the sea doesn't give me a second thought
as I stand on the cliff saluting
the breakers, watching the spindrift
cling to the sky a moment as if
salvation were there.

                    Salt collects
on my eyelids, my forehead, and I feel the fog
seeping into my mind, turning it greyer—
feathers of nothing, the unanswered
distance in a cloud. . . .
                    The bells ring
and the dead are carried away
each Saturday, *El Rancho Grande*
on the radio in the groundskeeper's truck—
I move along, nothing to see here
beyond the dust we knew would settle
in our cuffs.
                    May the wind forgive me
my idleness, my trespasses and nonsense
delivered indiscriminately throughout
the afternoons as I drift along,
forgive me for walking in my socks
past the bone yard and never
crossing myself or looking over
my shoulder.
                    I acknowledged
each cloudbank, each image shadowed
on the horizons of my youth—
what other subject remains after all
the rose heads have been pruned,
after the whitecaps' empty interjections?
The cloudy light of evening, and later,
a few ribbons of starlight? Nevertheless,
I breathe with all the dark silences
out there, singing—for no good reason
I can think of—together.

El Cielo

> *Adentro de la luz*
> *circula tu alma*
> *aminorandose hasta que se extingue*
> —Neruda

I have an understanding with the sky—
    each day I attend
the capitulation of the waves back into the blue
    and don't complain
too much . . . we look less and less like ourselves
    thought it's still us inside.
Youth gone, the knotted string of middle age, all up
    in the air like laundry
In a breeze, until we barely see ourselves disappearing
    in the swirl of dusk,
drifting toward a distant small town. . . . But on the way
    there, we're happy
to find a stool at the counter in a roadside café, drink
    a tepid cup of decaf,
a wink of cream added for what passes for luxury these days.
    The closer I come to the sky,
the more I want to believe that this is not it—that I'm still headed
    somewhere, anywhere at all. . . .

    *

In the park overlooking the sea, I sit beneath
    coral and eucalyptus trees
and breathe deeply alongside the crows—it's free,
    and the company, though ruffled,
is reliable, all of us bemused, looking into the aimless sky. . . .
    I set my pack down

and pour a cup of pinot noir, firs sip as balanced as
        the blue evening humming
out there above the island's edge. A second taste
        almost transcendental
as I send my *saludos* to the clouds who'll hedge my bets
        that it's just the evening mist
shifting around up there, and not angels who've overlooked
        their assignments here.
Tomorrow, I'll take another stab at making some sense
        of this . . . but in any event,
Caramba, it was fun as it flashed by. Might as well
        put more red poppies
and geraniums on the balcony and cheer the air up a bit.

        *

No fall, no winter—my shirtsleeves whip in a Santa Ana
        10 months out of 12
it seems, and like the trees, I'm a bit unsteady, exposed
        here on the cliff
in one of my dozen Hawaiian shirts picked up at the thrifts—
        all cotton, old school
surfers on long boards at Diamond Head, sail fish in the air,
        hibiscus flowers and coconut palms
swaying in that 60's light still fading at the Pacific's edge. . . .

        Hernandez warned us
about the tree of impossible things, and though I believed him
        I climbed branch by branch
as high as I could. I read philosophy in my 20s and understood
        that I didn't have much to say,
but wanted to say it anyway. . . . And though I've never imagined
        my heart as a frozen orange,
or a burning pomegranate there still might be something
        to the soul layered like an onion,
that dust cloud sifting down. . . . I'm out here working
        every day to unpuzzle

the mockingbird's oratorio to life, the *coplas* of spice finches
        congratulating each other
at the feeder as they hang on in the off shore breeze . . .
        I've found 100 ways to fear
death as much as anyone, and have hidden them in the silk trees,
        wrapped them in the froth
of breakers along the shore before the dark catches me out
        in the damp air, that,
nevertheless, keeps me, saves me from the stars, from our imminent
        relapse into dust
glimmering above the sea, where not one prayer has kept
        those birds in the air.

        *

    (for good Pablo)

The cypress take their shapes from the wind, grow old,
        and like our minds
sketch a poetics of emptiness. Yet in the leaf-green
        and lacy shade
of pepper trees, I think of you maestro, *compañero*,
        and call you back
from the solar mists, from the winds blowing toward
        the empty rooms
of eternity. Step out from the ribs and arm bones of your odes,
        say death means less than
the undertow murmuring in the tide, singing for nothing
        in our blood. Give us a *grito*
or two for the resistance, to chase the politicos over the cliff
        a song to repair the back ache,
the stitch in the side, numbness in the leg. Give us a trail
        of sea foam, crusts of sunlight
leading beyond the white caps that reveal the irony
        of every wasted appeal.
No one is fooled when we lose one comrade after another,
        when every breeze

miscalculates the sorrow of abandoned sidewalks
        and dead rose canes.
If we praise our shoes, or the two tomato plants
        we raise each spring,
if we proclaim a dishtowel the happy flag of our republic,
        even these scraps
of joy blow away through the blue leaves of evening—
        as the light goes out
across the shore, inside of which the soul spins
        Down and is gone . . .
the air-sealed kiss of salt in spindrift lost above the sea.

Walking Around

Yo paseo con calma, con ojos, con zapatos,
con furia, con olvido
—Neruda

When I get to the corner
the street lamp's still broken,
black wires hanging up there
like the entrails of a star.
When I wet my finger
and hold it up—the forecast is
for dust, more dust any day
you choose. . . .
              I get out early,
arm in arm with the shadows
before they dissolve
into thin air, heat
ascending the bluffs.
If there's a sliver or two
of cloud above the horizon,
above the inexhaustible
solitude I sometimes share
with the sea,
it's just a little punctuation
on the blank sheet of the blue,
some starred complaints
on the wind's inscrutable list,
a little nagging
from our fate that's
not about to change.

Some mornings
a heavy fog pulls
on my shoulder bones,
my hamstrings singing
out each time I bend

to admire the day lilies.
It's no use wondering
where the time has gone,
or the lilacs, the loquats,
the yellow blossoms
on the tipuana trees—
as far as metaphysics
are concerned, there's only
that itch at the back of my neck,
the spindrift tossed up
from the rocks,
the backdrop of what
still looks like oblivion
from here.   Downtown,
restaurants crowd the sidewalks
with little iron tables and chairs
for tourists to be seen eating
their salads. It's difficult
not to bump my knee
or slip to the curb as I pass,
my brain still trying
to account for the old
store fronts—the news agent's
selling El Productos, Dutch Masters,
the used book shop,
its musty caverns,
drilling light through shafts
of dust and time . . .
on the corners, Silverwoods,
Woolworths, Montgomery Wards. . . .

Once I thought
I saw my father at the
cracked Formica counter
in that tiny coffee shop
on Carrillo, and I still see
my mother standing
on State Street, in front

of the displays at Lou Rose,
window shopping for nothing
she can afford. . . .
     The air's
stretched thin from the silted
windowsills to the shore,
to some point on the horizon
where I just can't see
any further. . . .
     I want to shout
to the bus driver, the panhandlers,
the passersby, STOP,
I've had it up to here
with everyone forgetting!
But I stroll on sensibly
down the street
like a retired building inspector
still looking for cracks
and water stains—
recalling what I can
before the bits and pieces
of memory's ladder crumble
and the light burns up
with the useless supplications
of the leaves, the dust of space,
the spokes of the stars,
the near or far intervals
of silence everything slips
away to. . . .
     I'll get there
when I get there—and if
there's a moment to spare,
who knows where it is?
I'm just shuffling along
in my old coat and shoes,
nothing in my arms,
not even the fanfare of birds,
all which make me
finally even with the sky. . . .

Soy el mismo hasta ahorra

la vida es solo lo que hace
—Neruda

Each day the white lines of surf
re-write the shore . . .
I am 4, or 6, or 68,
I am called Cree, Crisco, Cristobal,
but I am still the same so far. . . .
I look out past the waves
and see my doubts
have never changed—
standing at the edge
of the shore, the world,
the updrafts of air, I am
only a little less bewildered
each time.
         Certainly
I never expected brilliance
to appear at my fingertips
like the burnt-orange blossoms
of honeysuckle in July
suddenly above the fence,
or like the flaming images
from his odes. But as a marker,
a memento of desire, I still see
Pablo's face in that photo
glowing before his walls of books,
beneath the clear-eyed figureheads
from 19th century ships
that sang the sea winds to him
each night . . . on his desk, agates
arranged in the lost alphabet
of the tides, polished by salt
and the glorious friction of the sun.

Phil gave me a fountain pen
an OMAS, a clear plastic demonstrator
through which I can see
the sky-blue cartridge, the ink-smudged
nib swirled like an ocean storm—
very much like the Sheaffers
nuns made us use for Penmanship
in school
        where I spent years copying
out the clouds in my notebook, capital **S**s
and **G**s with loops like the tops of cumulus
suspended over the channel, my sprawl
of cursive in blue on white, vague
and streaky as the afternoons
where I wrestled the nimbostratus,
opened my arms to the hard work
of hope.
        I still have notebooks,
pages yellow as September leaves
that tell me something I never fully
understand, especially now
when I find myself, as the old song says,
. . . just breezin' along with the breeze . . .

So I look around and make things up
to stand for what's lost all about me—
life is what life is about—
and if I had a choice, I'd choose to live
in this world; and if I didn't,
wouldn't I still be there in my 20s,
wearing my dead step father's
sport coat, a moth bitten black and white
herring bone blurring to grey
like everything else back there?

A few clouds settle above the islands,
mist low in the channel,
and I know as much as I ever did
about where we came from . . .
I'm just sitting here with a few twigs
of philosophy to rub together for warmth,
for comfort against the stars.
                              What I believe
this afternoon, I believed 60 years ago,
though the less essential bits shift
like a scrum of dust motes suspended
in sunlight.
              Each time I stop
and count to ten, I don't understand
anything more, I don't calm down.
You can travel the world, but finally
there's no where to go but home
to the sea. I don't know what
to make of the sandstone boulders
that haven't changed in centuries
for all my attention, my casual devotion.
It's still like that. I have this
little time to sit and admire the blue,
before I return to whatever I was
before I was here.

Christopher Buckley's *STAR JOURNAL: SELECTED POEMS* was published by the Univ. of Pittsburgh Press in 2016. Among several critical collections and anthologies of contemporary poetry, he has edited: *A Condition of the Spirit: The Life and Work of Larry Levis*, 2004, with Alexander Long; *Bear Flag Republic: Prose Poems and Poetics from California*, 2008, and *ONE FOR THE MONEY: The Sentence as a Poetic Form*, from Lynx House Press, 2012, both with Gary Young. He is the editor of *Homage to Vallejo*, 2006; *On the Poetry of Philip Levine: Stranger to Nothing*, 1991, and *FIRST LIGHT: A Festschrift for Philip Levine on his 85th Birthday*, 2013. *Messenger to the Stars: a Luis Omar Salinas New Selected Poems & Reader* was published in Tebot Bach's Ash Tree Poetry Series, 2014, and was edited with Jon Veinberg.

His poetry has appeared in *APR, POETRY, FIELD, The Georgia Review, The Iowa Review, TriQuarterly, The Kenyon Review, Ploughshares, The New Yorker, The Nation, The Hudson Review, The Gettysburg Review, Quarterly West, Prairie Schooner, The Southern Review, Five Points, New Letters, The Harvard Review,* and *Zyzzyva*.

His books of creative nonfiction are *Cruising State: Growing up in Southern California*, Univ. of Nevada Press, 1994; *SLEEP WALK*, Eastern Washington Univ. Press, 2006; and *Holy Days of Obligation*, Lynx House Press, 2014.

He is the recipient of a Guggenheim Fellowship in Poetry, two NEA grants, a Fulbright Award in Creative Writing, and four Pushcart Prizes. He was awarded the James Dickey Prize for 2008 from *FIVE POINTS* Magazine, the William Stafford Prize in Poetry for 2012 from *Rosebud*, and was the 2013 winner of the Campbell Corner Poetry Contest. His 20th book, *Back Room at the Philosophers' Club*, was the winner of the 2015 Lascaux Prize in Poetry.

He lives in Santa Barbara, CA with his wife, the artist, Nadya Brown, where he edits the poetry journal *MIRAMAR*.